The Big Sports Recipe Book

A collection of recipes from Sports Stars
in aid of The Prince's Trust

The Big Sports Recipe Book

A collection of recipes from Sports Stars in aid of The Prince's Trust

First published in 2012 by
Bene Factum Publishing Ltd
PO Box 58122
London
SW8 5WZ

Email: inquiries@bene-factum.co.uk

www.bene-factum.co.uk

ISBN: 978-1-903071-50-2

Every effort has been made to ensure that recipes in this book are the contributors' own work and that we have obtained the appropriate permissions.

In the history of cooking there really are very few recipes that haven't already been written or tweaked by previous cooks galore. We apologise if we appear to have used someone else's recipe, but all our contributors have tried to make their recipe original to themselves. There is no deliberate intention to infringe any copyrights. Please remember that this is a not for profit book, the recipes have been received by the publisher and sponsors in good faith, and the companies involved have given their service at cost or at zero cost because at the end of the day this project is for the benefit of The Prince's Trust to help change young lives.

A CIP catalogue record of this is available from the British Library.

Design and typesetting by www.creativetriangle.co.uk

Printed and bound by Geoff Neal Litho.

Acknowledgements

We would like to thank the following people for their invaluable help and effort. Without them this book would never have made it into your hands. They are:

Lafarge UK Ltd for providing the stage to sing.

Namita Patel and The Prince's Trust. You really do change lives.

Jo McBean, Jamie Brutnall and all the team at Creative Triangle, your creativity is second to none.

Annette Duckett & Ian Hemsworth.
One day we shall meet...

Geoff Neal Litho for all the printing. Great effort guys!

Anthony Weldon at Bene Factum.

Kim and her team at Tideswell School of Food for two great days in your hands. Thank You.

All at Lafarge who helped with their contacts and ideas.

Tristin Poyser & Suelen Wong. Amazing photographers.

Thanks to Sally David for all her advice on recipe books.

We cannot create a list of this significance without a massive thank you to our sports stars, their agents and their clubs. Thanks for taking the time to help others.

Lastly, to our close friends, colleagues, line managers and partners who kept the faith.

Thank You

James, Angela, Steve and David

The Winning Recipe Team

Contents

Foreword

Dion Dublin

Prince's Trust Ambassador

I have been involved with The Prince's Trust for 15 years and have seen first hand how young people can overcome significant barriers and go on to lead happier and more successful lives.

I am proud to be a Prince's Trust Ambassador and support a charity which makes such a difference to the lives of disadvantaged young people. The Prince's Trust Million Makers Corporate Challenge sees teams of employees from companies across the UK compete to turn a seed funding investment into a profit, by implementing and promoting their own mini enterprise. The 'Winning Recipes Team' at Lafarge chose to produce a cookbook of sport stars' recipes that hold a special significance to their creators; recipes they associate with winning, including my very own soup!

Currently there are more than one million young people in the UK who are not 'winning' and are facing their own challenges in life. The Prince's Trust strives to help these young people every day but can only give this much needed help with the funds that are generated by activities such as the Million Makers Challenge.

Through this book, we want to show more young people that with the support of The Prince's Trust, they can turn their lives around, as Khadija, Lee and Scott have done (see details of their stories, along with their own recipes on pages 64, 68 and 94). It's all about enjoying winning sporting moments, winning recipes and most importantly giving disadvantaged young people that 'winning feeling' which will help give them the skills and confidence to get into work, education or training.

Bon appetit!

The Prince's Trust

The Prince's Trust supports disadvantaged young people aged 13 to 30 by giving practical and financial support to those who need it most. They help young people who are long term unemployed, those who have struggled at school, offenders and ex-offenders and those who have been through the care system.

Through a range of tailored programmes, they help individuals to overcome personal barriers and develop key skills, confidence and motivation, enabling them to move into work, education or training. The Prince's Trust will help 50,000 disadvantaged young people this year and to do this need to raise almost £1 million a week.

For more information on The Prince's Trust please visit: www.princes-trust.org.uk

Aaron Ramsey

Football

Quick and healthy salmon linguine

One of the most promising midfielders in the Premier League, Aaron signed for Arsenal from Cardiff, (where he had played as a schoolboy) in the summer of 2008 for £5 million.

Aaron has represented Wales at Under 17 and Under 21 level and now has twenty senior caps to his name, scoring five goals. He was named as the youngest ever Wales Captain in March 2011 ahead of a game against England.

Ingredients

Serves 2 people

1 large (or 2 small) pre-cooked kiln roasted salmon fillets (available in supermarkets or alternatively you can use smoked salmon or tinned red salmon)

100g linguine (or your favourite pasta) – should be roughly a bunch the size of a 50 pence piece per person

½ white onion - finely chopped

1 garlic clove - finely chopped

1 handful of fresh basil leaves

150g broccoli

2 – 3 anchovy fillets in olive oil
(leave out if you don't like anchovies)

Grated parmesan cheese

Extra virgin olive oil to serve

Salt and cracked black pepper

Method:

Put a saucepan of water on to boil. When it has reached boiling point add the linguine, broccoli and some salt. Remove the broccoli after four minutes of cooking and set aside. Cook the pasta for ten minutes in total or until al dente and drain.

Meanwhile, heat a large frying pan and when hot, add a little olive oil. Fry the onions, garlic and anchovies on a low heat until the anchovies have melted away and the onions are translucent.

Then add the pre-cooked broccoli and the drained linguine and toss in the pan.

Flake the salmon fillets into the frying pan along with the grated parmesan and chopped basil leaves.

Serve warm topped with a little more parmesan and a drizzle of extra virgin olive oil.

Adam Jones

Rugby Union

Beer battered cod, chips and minted mushy peas

Beer battered cod, chips and minted mushy peas… my secret to amazing peas is bicarbonate of soda!

I love to eat the above meal after winning a game, whether it be an Ospreys or Welsh International.

Ingredients

Serves 4 people

Beer battered cod

950ml vegetable oil for frying

4 fillet cods – season with salt and pepper to taste

2 tbsp sea salt and 2 tbsp cayenne pepper (or to taste)

60g plain flour

1 egg beaten

150ml – good beer

Homemade cooked chips – in the oven

250g Maris Piper potatoes – or as many as you'd like!

75ml cooking oil

(Or could deep fat fry instead)

Minted mushy peas

5 sprigs of fresh mint – finely chopped

Salt and black pepper to taste

40g unsalted butter, in cubes and slightly softened

150ml water

200g frozen peas

Bicarbonate of soda

Method:

Heat the oil in a deep fat fryer to 190°C, season the cod with salt and pepper.

Mix the flour, salt, pepper and stir the egg mixture, gradually pour and mix the beer into this until a thin batter is formed.

Dip cod fillets into batter, one at a time and then put straight into the deep fat fryer and turn once until the cod is a golden colour.

Drain and serve!

Scrub the potatoes and cut into thick chunky chips (don't peel them) and then rinse in cold water.

Remove excess water and rub the oil over the chips, so all are covered.

Put on the oven at 200°C for about forty-five minutes, turn a couple of times.

Cook peas with water on a medium heat with half a teaspoon of salt, covered, although stir occasionally (approx seven minutes) until peas are tender.

In the meantime, stir the butter, mint and add the salt and pepper.

Once the peas are cooked, stir the mixture in and leave on medium heat for a couple of minutes.

Amir Khan

Boxing

Hot chicken curry

Since winning the Silver medal at the 2004 Olympics, Amir Khan has become one of Britain's best ever boxers.

He has an impressive professional fighting record; having become the World Light Welterweight Champion in July 2009 after his life changing fight with Andreas Kotelnik.

He hopes you think his meal is a knock out!

Ingredients

Serves 2 - 3 people

1 whole chicken

3 onions

2 tbsp red chilli powder

1 tbsp salt

¼ tbsp haldi (turmeric)

2 tsp garam masala

1 tsp mathee (dried fenugreek)

2 cloves garlic grated

1 inch ginger

2 tbsp vegetable oil

Fresh coriander

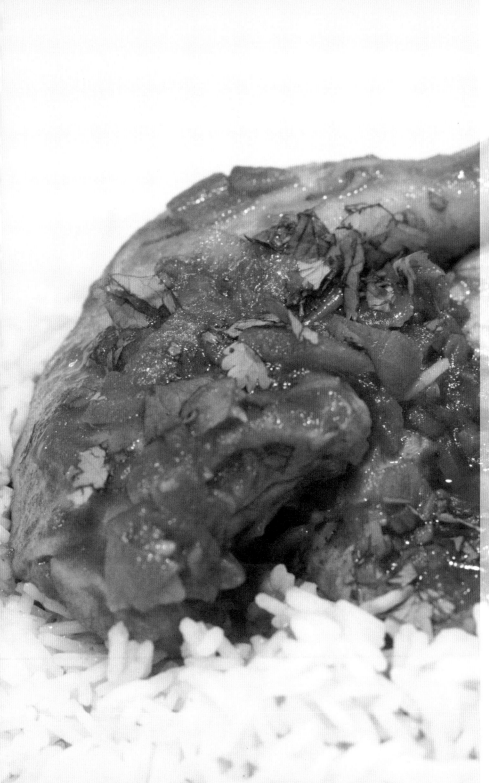

Method:

Chop the onions as normal, not too fat and not too thin, add to a deep frying pan and pour in two big glasses of water.

Add the chilli powder, salt and haldi, then cook for ten minutes until the onions start getting soft.

Get a wooden spoon and mash until they become very small. Once the water begins to reduce, add vegetable oil (roughly half a glass), garlic, and then add a teaspoon of garam masala, a tablespoon of mathee and also a small piece of ginger which needs to be mashed.

Keep stirring for five minutes then add the chicken into it. Make sure to keep stirring and adding water when you think it's getting kind of dry, but don't let it dry or you won't have any masala!

Keep checking and stirring it for at least twenty to thirty minutes then put 800ml of water in it so the chicken is almost drowning.

Put the lid on it and let it boil for ten minutes. Then give it a stir and add in some coriander. Leave it to simmer for a few minutes and then it's all done!

Serve with fresh pilau rice.

Annabel Croft

Tennis

Fillet of beef with soy sauce

Annabel Croft is one of the best female tennis players the UK has known. She has won the Wimbledon and Australian Open girls tournaments and also the Virginia Slims of San Diego tournament .

In her career, she achieved a world ranking of twenty-one and played for Great Britain in the Fed Cup and Wightman Cup.

Ingredients

Serves 4 people

Meat

1kg beef fillet

Marinade

½ cup olive oil

½ cup light soy sauce

Juice from 1 medium sized lemon

Big knob of ginger grated

2 small red chillies chopped

Oyster sauce optional
(but I did put a big splash in)

Fish sauce

Method:

Create the marinade by mixing half a cup each of the soy sauce and oil and then adjust the rest of the ingredients to your taste.

Coat the beef in marinade and place in the fridge for thirty minutes.

Preheat oven to 190°C. Heat the oil in a flameproof roasting pan on the stove over medium-high heat. Sear the beef for one to two minutes on each side. Transfer to the oven and roast for twenty to twenty-five minutes for medium-rare (or until done to your liking). Rest beef for ten minutes.

Serve with noodles and vegetables of your choice.

Beth Storry

Hockey

Broccoli, chicken and cashew nut stir fry

Beth tried her hand at ballet and gymnastics before turning her hand to hockey.

Her former acrobatic sports should help her in the position of goal-keeper! Beth was outstanding in goal for GB at the 2008 Beijing Olympic Games.

Ingredients

Serves 2 people

1 tbsp soy sauce

2 tsp seasoned rice vinegar or white wine vinegar

Juice of 1 small orange

1 tsp dark muscovado sugar

2 tsp cornflour

2 tbsp stir-fry oil or vegetable oil

85g unsalted cashews nuts

1 medium onion, thinly sliced

1 large skinless boneless chicken breast fillet, cut into chunks

250g broccoli florets

150g pack mangetout, sliced in half

1 red pepper, seeded and thinly sliced

Method:

In a jug, mix together the soy sauce, vinegar, orange juice, muscovado sugar and cornflour. Set aside.

Heat the oil in a wok. Add the cashews and cook for a minute until golden brown. Quickly remove the nuts and tip on to kitchen paper to drain. Add the onion slices and fry over a high heat for three to five minutes until browned and softened, then lift them out and add to the cashews.

Tip the chicken into the wok and stir fry for three to four minutes, then tip in the broccoli, mangetout and red pepper and stir fry for another four to five minutes until the vegetables are tender yet still crunchy.

Stir the cornflour mixture to blend the ingredients, pour into the wok and stir fry for a couple of minutes until the sauce thickens. Stir in the onion and cashews, then pile on to warm plates.

Beth Storry

Hockey

Beth's brownies

The brownies are not part of my diet!
However, I love baking for my friends and
family outside of hockey and it would be a
very occasional treat for me and the team to
have something like this!

Ingredients

55g cocoa

50ml boiling water

85g butter

225g sugar

1 egg, beaten

½ tsp vanilla essence

100g flour

½ tsp baking powder

100g chocolate chunks
(big chunks, white, pure, with hazelnuts)

Method:

Preheat oven to 180°C.

Grease baking tray.

Mix cocoa, water, melted butter and stir well.

Add sugar, vanilla and egg and stir well.

Sieve the flour and baking powder and stir.

Stir in the chocolate chunks.

Mix until smooth.

Bake for about twenty-five minutes
(check with your finger, but remember
this may be hot. If too soft, then go for
another five minutes).

Voila!

Chris Pilgrim

Rugby Union

Pancakes

I have this meal for breakfast on the day of matches as a bit of a ritual, it started from when I had it the morning of the day when Newcastle won the JP Morgan 7s and I scored the winning try in the final.

Ingredients

3 whole eggs

120g fine oat flour

1 heaped tsp of baking powder

140ml milk

Pinch of salt

Method:

Separate the eggs, whites in one bowl and the yolks in another.

Add the milk to the egg yolks, followed by the sieved flour and baking powder. Mix together to form a smooth batter which should be quite thick.

Add the pinch of salt to the egg whites and then whisk until stiff peaks are formed.

Fold the batter into the whites being careful to mix well without knocking too much of the air out of them.

Heat a non-stick pan (I find a small omelette pan a good size) over a medium heat and pour one quarter of the batter in. Fry for a couple of minutes until golden brown, turn and cook the other side until cooked through.

Colin Jackson

Athletics – Hurdles

Spicy coconut chicken

This recipe is one that I used on Masterchef. I cooked it for my family as a practice and they said I should use it on Masterchef, so I did!

Ingredients

2 skinless chicken breasts

2 dashes soy sauce

2 tsp sugar

Rice

Place in a blender...

1 tsp dried chilli flakes

1 tbsp chopped peanuts

½ tsp black peppercorns

2 stems of lemon grass

4 spring onions

1 ½ tins of coconut milk

½ tsp shrimp paste

...and liquidise

Leave it to rest for ten minutes

Method:

Fry the chicken in a large pan with a little oil until brown. Add two dashes of soy sauce and add two teaspoons of sugar. Keep frying and turning the chicken so that it has an even coat of the soy sugar juice.

Pour the mixture from the blender into the pan with the chicken and bring to boil. Turn down the heat, and simmer for twenty minutes, remove until the chicken is tender and cooked through.

Serve with steamed rice.

Colin Turkington

Touring Cars

Thai chicken curry

This is probably my favourite dish but also a healthy, but tasty meal prior to, or after a race meeting. Leading up to a race this is the type of food I would eat along with rice and naan bread. For me there is a good mix of protein and carbohydrate.

After a race, I would also eat this but maybe replace the rice with chips. After the hard work of a race weekend, I always fancy something a little naughty.

Ingredients

For the spice paste

1 inch fresh ginger coarsely chopped

2 lime leaves chopped

3 shallots peeled and chopped

A bunch of coriander stalks finely chopped

4 red chillies de-seeded and finely chopped

1 tsp ground turmeric

1 tsp sugar

2 lemongrass stalks, dry outer layers removed, inner core finely chopped

2 tbsp fish sauce

3 garlic cloves peeled and chopped

For the Curry

3 tbsp vegetable oil

12 boned chicken thighs roughly chopped

250ml chicken stock

Method:

Blend all of the spice paste ingredients in a food processor to make a paste. If a little dry, add vegetable oil in dribbles.

Slice chicken and fry in oil until the outside is cooked, then add paste and cook for five minutes to heat paste through.

Now add stock and cook until chicken is thoroughly cooked and then simmer to reduce sauce slightly.

Dan Greaves

Athletics – Discus

Roast gammon with mixed veg and sweet potatoes

Dan has always been a keen sportsman, first trying his hand in the hammer throw as a schoolboy, showing early signs of potentially competing as a representative for his county.

It was his staggering physique and unquestionable power that paved the way for him to field his potential as a discus thrower. At the Sydney Paralympics in 2000, Dan made his presence known on the international circuit. At the age of just 18, he threw himself to a podium place taking the silver medal in his F44/46 category. Four years on at the Paralympics in Athens, he was to go that one step further and throw a distance that saw him crowned Paralympic champion, grabbing the gold medal and setting the world record with a throw of 55.53m.

2008 saw Dan return to the Paralympics again in a bid to retain his title. Despite a podium finish, the fact that he returned 'disappointed' with a bronze is testament to Dan's mentality as an athlete who strives for the best.

Ingredients

2 kg boneless gammon joint

Handful of whole cloves

80g honey

40g brown sugar

4 tbsp olive oil

1 tbsp ground cumin

750g sweet potatoes – peeled and cubed

Mixed vegetables of your choice

Method:

Boil the gammon and simmer for one and a half hours, then cool on a chopping board.

Heat up the honey and sugar until the sugar dissolves for the glaze.

Score the fat on the gammon in a diamond pattern and place whole cloves into the scores. Glaze the honey mixture over the gammon and bake in a preheated oven at 200°C for forty-five minutes, basting frequently. Rest for at least fifteen minutes before carving.

For the sweet potatoes, mix the oil and cumin together and pour over the potatoes. Place in the oven at 200°C for about fifteen minutes or until tender.

David Gillick

Athletics – 400 metres

Breakfast pancake

David was the first Irish man to make a World Final.

He specialises in the 400m and won the European Indoor Championships Gold Medal in 2005 and 2007. He set the Irish indoor record of 45.52 seconds in the 2007 final. The time also beat the Irish outdoor record of 45.58 and was within the Olympic 'A' qualifying standard for the 2008 games.

Ingredients

Per person

60g oats

25g whey

1 egg (medium free range)

½ tsp baking powder

1 tsp / 4g coconut oil

70g 5% Greek yoghurt

50g berries

Water

You'll also need

Microwave

Microwavable bowl

Frying pan

Method:

Place oats in a microwavable bowl and add enough water to just cover them.

Place the bowl in a microwave and cook for thirty seconds on the highest setting.

Take the bowl out and add egg, whey, baking powder and then mix.

Heat the coconut oil in a large non-stick frying pan and evenly distribute it (if you have excess liquid from the coconut oil, soak it up with kitchen towel).

Add pancake mixture to the frying pan and evenly distribute.

When one side of the pancake is cooked, flip it over to cook the other – your pancake is ready to flip if you can scoop your spatula under the pancake.

When ready, carefully transfer your pancake from frying pan to the centre of your plate. Add yoghurt and fruit and serve!

David Moorcroft

Athletics – Distance Runner

Date loaf

I first had date loaf at a friend's home in Hamilton, New Zealand in 1977. My wife Linda and I went to teach in New Zealand in August 1977. At the time I had a bad back injury and had hardly raced since I competed in my first Olympic Games in Montreal 1976.

Whilst teaching at St Pauls Collegiate School in Hamilton, I had the support and friendship of the athletics community there. The staff at the school enabled me to get back into running again and I went on to win the Commonwealth Games in 1978.

Our friends there, Jim and Liz Eveleigh and their family were a great support. Liz baked this cake which she believed fired me up with the energy that I needed to train as hard as I did!

Ingredients

Part 1

½lb dates

¾lb butter

1 tsp soda

Part 2

6oz sugar

8oz plain flour

You'll also need

1 loaf tin - medium sized

Greaseproof paper

Method:

Cover part 1 with one cup of boiling water –
allow to cool.

Add part 2 and beat a little.

Pour into prepared greaseproof tins.

Bake at 180˚C for forty-five minutes to
an hour.

Derek White

Rugby Union

Scottish Grand Slam salmon parcels

This is a meal to be enjoyed all year round but it really becomes spectacular when the vegetables are in season. Having a father who was a keen fisherman certainly helped with the supply of salmon or, more often, sea trout. However even when his luck was out, the quality you could get from the local fishmongers or supermarkets in Edinburgh was very good.

I often made these parcels during the time I played for Scotland. It was just before the sport went professional and I had to balance the demands of a full time job and the rigours of a heavy training schedule.

Nutrition was extremely important to ensure I could maintain fitness and this ticked all the boxes for nutrition, taste, convenience, speed and of course very little washing-up! It is a meal that reflected the Scottish team at that time – the finest of Scottish ingredients but also influenced by other nationalities and cultures. However, unlike the team then - this was a winner everytime!

Ingredients

Fillet of Scottish salmon

4-6 stalks of asparagus tips

Handful of cherry tomatoes

1 tsp olive oil

Fresh spinach

Lemon juice or white wine

Handful of new potatoes

Method:

Heat oven to 220°C for twenty to twenty-five minutes.

On a square piece of foil, build a stack starting with the asparagus tips, spinach and tomatoes. Top with a well peppered fillet of salmon. Drizzle with oil and add lemon juice or white wine if you have a bottle open (we usually do!).

Wrap and fold to seal and cook for twenty to twenty-five minutes. Serve with new potatoes.

Experiment with other veg such as broccoli spears or blanched green beans.

Dion Dublin

Football – Prince's Trust Ambassador

Red lentil soup with lemon yoghurt

Dion was capped four times for England, and during an illustrious club career that saw him star at both centre forward and centre back, he played for Norwich City, Cambridge United, Manchester United, Coventry City, Millwall, Aston Villa, Leicester City and Celtic.

Since retiring, Dion has gone on to become a favourite Football Pundit regularly appearing on programmes for both Sky Sports and the BBC. He is also known as an accomplished percussionist and has even invented a percussion instrument which he named "The Dube".

Ingredients

1 tbsp olive oil

1 onion finely chopped

½ tbsp grated ginger

2 carrots diced

2 celery stalks chopped

1 red pepper chopped

2 garlic cloves grated

1 red chilli seeded and finely sliced

400g canned tomatoes whole or chopped

2 tbsp tomato puree

100g red lentils

1.5l vegetable stock mixed with hot water

Chopped parsley and a few sprigs for decorative purposes

1 tbsp greek yoghurt

1 lemon juiced and grated

Method:

Heat the oil in a large pan. Cook the onion, carrots, celery and red pepper for about five minutes or until it begins to soften.

Add ginger, garlic, tomato puree and chilli and cook for a further few minutes.

Add tinned tomatoes, lentils and vegetable stock and bring to the boil. Reduce the heat and simmer for forty-five minutes.

Stir in chopped parsley. To serve, add greek yoghurt mixed with a splash of fresh juice of lemon juice and rind with lemon and grated zest.

Dylan Hartley
Rugby Union

Thai green curry

Dylan Hartley is currently Captain of Northampton Saints and is a full England International.

He is one of the very few players to score a test try only three minutes after stepping off the bench but did so with gusto when winning his twentieth cap, against New Zealand at Twickenham in 2010.

For Northampton Saints, he became the youngest captain in the Premiership when leading the Saints in the 2009-2010 season.

Ingredients

Serves 4 people

For the paste

4 small thai green chillies
(or thai medium paste)

1 small red onion cubed

1 stalk lemon grass chopped

1 inch ginger grated

1 tsp cumin

½ tsp ground coriander

1 tsp shrimp sauce

3 tbsp fish sauce

1 tsp white pepper
(use black if you can't get it)

2 tbsp lime juice

2 handfuls of fresh coriander

For the curry

2 tbsp vegetable oil

3 chicken breasts cut into pieces

1 can of coconut milk

Zest of 1 lime

2 red peppers de-seeded and cut into pieces

Handful of fresh basil

Method:

Place all items for the paste and blend in a processor until it forms a paste (or use about four teaspoons of bought paste).

Warm a wok (or large pan) on a high heat. When hot, add oil and leave for thirty seconds. Then add paste and stir up to a minute. Add three quarters of the coconut milk and add the chicken, keep stirring throughout.

Bring to the boil and reduce the heat to medium / low and leave to simmer with the lid on for about four minutes, stirring occasionally.

Add the red pepper and lime zest, on same heat still stirring continuously. Leave for about another four minutes.

Check the salt. If more salt is needed, add more fish sauce. If too spicy, then add more coconut milk.

Serve with rice. Garnish with basil and split the remaining coconut milk over the meals.

Ellie Koyander

Freestyle Mogul Skiing

Pecan crusted chicken and roast veggies

Hi, I'm Ellie Koyander and I'm a Freestyle Mogul Skier. My sport is one of the most exciting skiing disciplines which involves explosively skiing down a steep and bumpy terrain as fast as you can, whilst performing aerial manoeuvres such as a 'back flip' off the two jumps!

In 2010, I was the youngest member of Team GB at the Vancouver Winter Olympic Games and I currently travel the world, training and competing on the FIS Freestyle Mogul World Cup circuit. My current ambition is to win an Olympic Gold medal at the next Winter Olympics in 2014, and to push my sport to its limits!

Wherever I am in the world, I love to make this simple, healthy and tasty chicken dish. It's great as an energising lunch or dinner after a long day / competition and leaves you feeling refreshed and ready to conquer anything! The combination of mustard, pecans and honey makes a tangy yet sweet crust around the succulent chicken and when combined with the roasted vegetables, you are sure to be using my recipe for chicken from now on!

Follow my journey on Twitter to the 2014 Olympics and beyond at @elliekoyander.

But for now… enjoy!

Ingredients

Serves 3-4 people

4 chicken breasts

150g pecan nuts

180g French mustard

Carrots

Parsnips

Beetroot

Sweet potato

Onion

Red pepper and any of your favourite veggies

Olive oil for drizzling on the vegetables

2 tbsp honey

Method:

Pre-heat your oven to around 180°C.

Prepare all the vegetables and place in a large baking tray. I like to cut them into about one and a half inch chunks but it's really up to you how thick or thin you desire them to be.

Cover the vegetables with a light drizzle of olive oil and place the tray into the oven, setting a timer to check them in about thirty minutes time to give them a quick stir.

Place the pecans into a food processor and blend until nicely chopped with a few bigger pieces still in the mix. Place some pecans onto a plate and put the rest to one side until more pecans are needed on the plate as you begin rolling the mustard covered chicken.

Pour the mustard and two tablespoons of honey into a bowl, stirring until well combined to roll the chicken breasts in. Place next to the plate with the pecan nuts on.

Ensure you have a second baking tray ready to put the dunked and rolled chicken breasts on to.

Now prepare the chicken breasts by cutting off any excess fat and roll them in a paper towel to dry them off, so that the mustard mixture will stick more easily.

After patting dry, dunk a chicken breast into the mustard mixture on both sides and then roll it in the pecans, placing on the baking tray when ready. Repeat for the rest of the chicken breasts.

Place the chicken into the oven on the top shelf and if the timer for the vegetables hasn't gone off yet, pull them out and give them a quick stir and leave in the oven until the chicken is ready.

The chicken will need to bake for around twenty-five to forty minutes, depending on the size of the breast and your oven. You will know when it is ready by cutting into the thickest breast and having the juices run clear with no 'pinkness' to the meat.

Serve one chicken breast per person, add a scoop or two of roasted veggies and voila-simple, delicious and succulent chicken… yum!

Geordan Murphy

Rugby Union

Fish pie

One of the most decorated men in club rugby and one of the most naturally gifted and popular in Leicester's long history, club captain Geordan Murphy began his 15th season with Tigers in 2011/12.

Murphy has seven league titles to his name, captaining Tigers to wins in the 2009 and 2010 finals after succeeding Martin Corry in that role.

The leading try-scorer in Tigers' Heinekėn Cup history, Murphy played in the finals of 2001, 2002, 2007 and also in 2009, when he led the team out as captain against Leinster.

Ingredients

Serves 4 people

5 large Maris Piper potatoes peeled and diced (about 3 cm)

Salt and pepper

2 free range eggs (leave out if you don't like)

2 handfuls of spinach (I used 1 x 200gms packet of baby spinach)

1 brown onion finely chopped

1 carrot chopped / diced

1 – 2 celery stalks finely chopped

Extra virgin olive oil

285ml cream

2 good handfuls of grated parmesan or cheddar cheese

Juice of 1 lemon

1 heaped tsp English mustard

1 large handful of flat leafed parsley, finely chopped

500g smoked haddock sliced into strips and then chopped into biggish chunks

Nutmeg (optional) - I added the nutmeg to my mash

Delicious home made Italian dishes, in a stylish setting, with new ownership by Leicester Tigers players Geordan Murphy and Martin Castrogiovanni in Leicester and Market Harborough.

Our dining experience fuses contemporary with traditional and offers an experience to satisfy all appetites. The atmosphere is laid back sophistication, whether you want an intimate meal or a group celebration, we are confident of our ability to cater for your needs.

Buon appetito!

Method:

Pre-heat oven to 220°C.

I chop all the ingredients, juice the lemon and prepare everything ready to cook.

Boil the potatoes in salted water for a couple of minutes.

Add the two eggs and set timer for eight minutes and add to the spuds. Remove the eggs when ready and cool, peel and cut into quarters.

Place a colander or sieve over the boiling potatoes and empty the spinach in, put the lid on and steam for about two minutes (how convenient). Remove and drain.

When the spuds are cooked, drain in the colander.

In a separate pan, fry the onion, celery and carrot for about five minutes in the olive oil, then add the cream and bring to the boil.

Remove from the heat, add the cheese, lemon juice, parsley and mustard – stir.

Mix the spinach (which you have squeezed and chopped up), the chopped up fish and egg into the cream mixture and then empty into an appropriately sized oven dish.

Mash up the potatoes with a drizzle of olive oil (or butter), salt and pepper and a few gratings of nutmeg and then lightly spread over the fish pie using a fork.

You could drizzle a bit more oil or melted butter over the top to get a browner finish, or sprinkle over some more cheese if you really wanted to be decadent and get some more crunch (if you were to do this, I would do it ten minutes before the end of the cooking time).

Bake for about twenty-five to thirty mins – until golden.

Hannah Miley

Swimming

Butterfly chicken

I have to admit I have two favorite meals I like to cook; lasagne and butterfly chicken with couscous :-)

Ingredients

1 chicken breast (filleted)

25g mozzarella cheese

1 – 2 rashers of bacon

A packet of couscous
(sadly I don't make my own couscous,
I use it straight from the packet)

Stir-fry veg (of your choice)

Method:

Take the chicken breast and slice in half so it opens out like a butterfly (don't slice the fillet completely in half!).

Slice the mozzarella cheese and place onto the opened out chicken.

Close the fillet and use the bacon to wrap around it.

Now wrap the chicken in tin foil and place in the oven at around 200°C.

Cook for around thirty-five to forty minutes, keep checking to ensure that the meat is cooked.

Whilst the chicken is cooking, prepare and make the couscous. My favourite is mushroom!

Prepare the veg to stir fry – I normally slice some spring onions and baby tomatoes and fry them with a little bit of garlic but any veg will do :-)

Imran Sherwani

Hockey

Spicy steak and chips

I do like a steak and my favourite method of cooking it is using a few ingredients to spice it up.

Ingredients

½ tsp chilli powder

½ tsp garlic powder

1 tip of ginger

Rib eye steak

Butter

Mushrooms

Home made chips – potatoes

Method:

Mix the chilli, garlic and ginger into a paste with a little water and smear the paste on both sides of the rib eye steak.

Allow to marinade.

Cook the steak on a high heat, sealing the meat on all edges and fat first. Then seal the meat on both sides keeping the heat high.

The key thing is to allow the steak to rest allowing the meat to relax, before serving with mushrooms and home made chunky chips.

Jack Wilshire

Football

Beef noodle stir-fry

This recipe is one of Jack's favourites. He picked it up from one of the chefs at Arsenal FC.

Ingredients

Serves 4

2 tsp vegetable oil

400g lean beef steak, sliced thinly

4 garlic cloves, crushed

2 yellow, red or green peppers, de-seeded and sliced

1 red and 1 white onion, sliced

100g mushrooms, finely sliced

200g beansprouts

4 tbsp soy sauce

4 tbsp sweet chilli sauce

Method:

Heat the oil in a non-stick frying pan or wok and add the beef.

Stir fry for one to two minutes to seal, then add the garlic, peppers, onions, mushrooms along with two tablespoons of water.

Continue to cook for about two minutes, then add the beansprouts, sweet chilli sauce and soy sauce and then add noodles (check packet instructions). Allow to heat through and serve immediately.

Jenson Button

Formula 1

Sticky toffee pudding

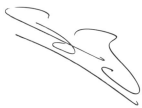

As a sportsman, I know that I need to look after my body – and that means training hard and eating well.

The Formula 1 season is so long nowadays that there's rarely a chance to relax, but I'm only human, and you can't always stick to the same regime – so sticky toffee pudding is the perfect way to reward myself. Usually, my diet is chicken or fish with salad, which is incredibly healthy. But if you see me with a plate of sticky toffee pudding, then you know it has been a good day.

Ingredients

Serves 6

For the cake

120g light muscovado sugar

175g self raising flour

150ml milk (full fat / semi)

1 egg

1 tsp vanilla extract

50g unsalted butter, melted

200g chopped, rolled dates (tip: soak them in boiling water before adding them, it makes them stickier!)

For the toffee sauce

100g unsalted butter, melted

2 tbsp golden syrup

100g light muscovado sugar

140ml double cream

To serve

6 ramekins – greased

Method:

Preheat the oven to 190°C / gas mark 5.

Combine the 100g brown sugar with the flour in a large bowl. In a separate bowl, pour the milk, beat in the egg, add the vanilla extract, melted butter and when smooth pour over into the flour and stir. Fold in the dates and then evenly spread to the ramekins. They should be ready in forty-five minutes.

To make the sauce, mix the butter, golden syrup, sugar and cream in a pan and put on a low heat until the sugar has dissolved, the sauce has thickened and gone a dark brown colour. Serve warm with the pudding and if feeling extra naughty serve with vanilla ice cream or crème fraiche.

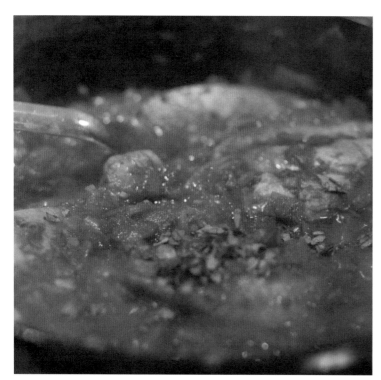

Jimmy Greaves

Football

The Notley bacon sandwich

Jimmy Greaves is one of the finest footballers of his generation. He is the man, the great Pele, once described as the most gifted goal scorer he had ever seen. Throughout his career Jimmy played for a number of clubs, most notably Chelsea, AC Milan and Tottenham Hotspur.

He is England's third highest ever goal scorer and the highest goal scorer in the history of the English top flight.

His 41 goals for Chelsea in the 1960-61 season remain an all-time club record.

In 1960, he became the youngest player to score 100 league goals in English football, at the age of 20 years 290 days.

Greaves played at Spurs from 1961 to 1970, scoring a club record of 266 goals in 379 matches, including 220 goals in the First Division. Greaves finished as top League goal scorer in 1963, 1964, 1965 and 1969. His record of finishing top goal scorer in six seasons has never been matched.

With Spurs, Jimmy won the FA Cup in 1962 and 1967, scoring against Burnley in the former final. He also won the European Cup Winners' Cup in 1963 – scoring twice in the 5-1 win over Atlético Madrid, ensuring that Spurs became the first British club to win a European trophy. Today he is considered one of the best players in the history of Tottenham Hotspur.

Ingredients

Serves 1

2 slices of thick cut granary bread

4 slices of thick cut back bacon – trim off fat

1 large egg (optional)

Method:

Cut the granary bread into thick slices.

Grill the back bacon to your liking.

Fry a fresh large egg. (optional)

Butter both pieces of bread.

Slap on the bacon.

Enjoy with a mug of freshly brewed tea!

PS, No sauce of any kind.

Joe Ledley

Football

Spicy Moroccan stewed fish with couscous

Joe signed for Scottish Premier League Champions Celtic from Cardiff, his home town team and where he had spent six years, in 2010.

Whilst at Cardiff, he helped the club to the FA Cup final in 2008 and to the Championship play-off final in 2010. At Celtic, he won the Scottish Cup in his first season with the club and helped in their bid for the 2011 / 2012 title.

Joe has represented Wales at Under 17, Under 19 and Under 21 levels, before making his full debut in 2005, since then he has been capped a total of 41 times scoring three goals.

Ingredients

Serves 2 people

2 cod fillets

50g prawns

2 cloves of garlic

1 tin of chopped tomatoes

1 red chilli

2 handfuls of fresh or frozen peas

1 fresh bunch of basil

1 tsp whole cumin seeds

1 lemon

Cinnamon

Olive oil

Salt and pepper

Method:

Put the couscous into a bowl and add a couple of teaspoons of olive oil. Halve the lemon and squeeze in the juice adding some salt and pepper. Pour in enough boiling water to cover the couscous, then cover with a plate or cling film. Leave for about ten minutes.

Get a large saucepan on medium heat. Peel and slice your garlic and chilli. Pick the basil leaves off the stalks. Put the smaller ones to one side and roughly slice the larger ones.

Add a couple of lugs to the hot pan.

Add garlic, chilli, basil, cumin seeds and cinnamon. Give it a stir and put the cod fillets on top. Scatter over the prawns. Add the tinned tomatoes and frozen peas. Put the lid on and bring to the boil, then turn the heat down to a simmer and cook for eight minutes or until the fish and prawns are cooked through and flake easily. Taste - and season accordingly with salt and pepper.

By the time the fish is cooked, the couscous should have soaked up the water and be ready to serve. Spoon the couscous into a large bowl and give it a stir with a fork to help it fluff up. Top with the fish, vegetables and juices from the pan and sprinkle with the reserved basil leaves.

Then tuck in!

Junior Hoilett

Football

Jerk chicken with rice and peas

David 'Junior' Hoilett made his first team debut for Blackburn Rovers in 2009. He quickly established himself as a first team regular.

His first competitive goal came in a 3-1 League Cup win against Gillingham in 2009.

The 2011/12 season has seen Junior establish himself as a key member of the Blackburn Rovers first team.

Ingredients

Serves 2 - 3 people

For the chicken

Vegetable oil for deep frying

12 chicken legs

200g / 7oz good quality jerk seasoning

For the rice and peas

50ml / 2 fl oz vegetable oil

1 onion finely chopped

300g / 10 oz long grain rice

400ml / 14 fl oz water

400ml / 14 fl oz coconut milk

400g / 14 oz tinned kidney beans rinsed and drained

3 tsp chopped fresh thyme

Fresh coriander leaves to serve

Serve with a dish of sweet potato or coleslaw

Method:

For the Jerk chicken, place the vegetable oil into a deep heavy bottomed saucepan and heat until a small cube of bread sizzles and turns golden when dropped in.

Place the chicken legs into a large bowl and dredge in the jerk seasoning to coat all over. Carefully place into the hot oil and deep fry, turning occasionally for about twelve minutes or until golden brown and completely cooked through. Remove from the oil with a slotted spoon and drain onto kitchen paper.

For the rice and peas, heat the oil in a large lidded pan and fry the onion until softened, but not coloured. Add the rice (un-cooked) and stir well, then add the water and bring to the boil.

Add the coconut milk, kidney beans and thyme, reduce the heat and simmer, covered for about twenty minutes, or until the rice is cooked. Season to taste with salt and freshly ground pepper.

Keri-Anne Payne

Swimming

Orange and poppy seed cake

I was asked on twitter if I had any good lemon drizzle recipes, I do have a few but I LOVE this twist on the old classic… an orange and poppy seed cake.

I hope you find this as tasty as I do, and if you do bake it, make sure you tweet a photo to me :) @keriannepayne

Ingredients

For the sponge

185g butter

1 orange

200g self-raising flour, sifted

80g plain flour

60g ground almonds

4 tbsp milk

25g poppy seeds

½ tbsp grated orange zest

½ tbsp grated lemon zest

3 eggs

110ml orange juice

20ml lemon juice

200g caster sugar

For the syrup

70ml orange juice

50ml water

½ peel of an orange

80g caster sugar

1 tbsp honey

Method:

Pre-heat the oven to 200°C / 180°C fan oven and grease a round (22cm) cake tin and line the bottom with grease proof paper.

Soak the poppy seeds in the milk.

Cream the butter, sugar, lemon and orange zest together until pale and fluffy. Add the eggs one at a time and beat well after each addition. Fold in the flours and the ground almonds, then stir in the orange and lemon juice along with the soaked poppy seed and milk mixture.

Pour the sponge mixture into the cake tin and bake in the middle of the oven for forty to forty-five minutes, or until golden brown. If you have a metal skewer, pierce the middle of the cake and if it comes out clean the cake is ready.

While the cake is baking you can make the syrup.

Add all the syrup ingredients, apart from the honey, to a small pan on a medium heat. When the sugar has dissolved add the honey and keep on the heat until the orange peel softens, approx five minutes.

Remove the cake from oven and leave it to cool for five minutes. Once the cake has cooled, remove it from the tin and transfer it to a wire rack. At this stage, pierce the cake with the skewer a few times to make holes for the syrup to run down. Place a plate underneath the cake and pour the syrup over the cake. Re-pour any syrup that has collected on the plate. This can be served warm or cold.

Khadija Osman

Prince's Trust supported young person – Enterprise

Chocolate coconut board with cherries

When Khadija Osman made the decision to leave college she had ambitions to make it in business. However, her plans were put on hold after a serious back injury, which left her virtually housebound for several months.

Undeterred, the 18 year old from Leicester, spent the time learning how to make chocolate with her mum.

Now, the young entrepreneur is beginning to taste success with her business, Chocolate Loves Chocolate.

Khadija set up the firm using a £1,700 loan from The Prince's Trust and produces hand-made sweet treats for events such as weddings and baby showers and is in talks with Leicester businesses about stocking her products.

Khadija said: "It's been amazing, things are going really well." When she had recovered from her back injury, Khadija applied to do work experience with an award-winning chocolatier. "I learnt so much including lots of tricks of the trade," said Khadija.

Khadija used The Prince's Trust loan to buy specialist chocolate making equipment, set up a website and rent and furnish a workshop and office space.

She said: "I wanted to be as careful with that money as if it was my own and I'm reinvesting the profits back into the business."

Ingredients

250g butter (preferably dairy free butter)

½ cup caster sugar

2 cups ready oats

4 tbsp Golden Syrup

250g of your favorite chocolate or Chocolate Loves Chocolate's chocolate / C.L.C Vegan Chocolate

1 cup desiccated coconut

2 tsp bicarbonate of soda

1 tbsp good quality Fairtrade cocoa

2 - 2 ½ cups plain flour

1 handful of cherries

Method:

Mix together the butter and caster sugar until smooth, add the golden syrup and beat for two minutes.

Add the rest of the ingredients (except the chocolate and cherries) to the bowl and combine with an electric whisk - SLOWLY - to form a soft dough. Roll out the dough to roughly 5mm thick and cut out into shapes preferably with an oval biscuit cutter.

Dent the biscuits in the centre with the back of a knife. Place the biscuits 2cm apart on an oven tray and bake at 180°C for ten to fifteen minutes or until golden brown and crisp; leave to cool on trays.

Melt the chocolate in a bowl suspended on top of a pot filled with boiling water. When biscuits are cool, sandwich them with the melted chocolate.

Place them onto a wooden board, scatter the cherries on top of them and serve.

Lauren Taylor

Golf

Fish curry

Image courtesy of Cal Carson
Golf Agency

Lauren Taylor is the BBC's Young Sports Personality of the Year 2011, the British Ladies Amateur Champion and an England International.

Here is my favourite quick curry recipe which we have at home and was adapted from a recipe by Jamie Oliver. It is really quick and easy, so any 17 year old can do this.

Ingredients

Serves 2 people

3 heaped tbsp pre-made curry paste

2 portions (180g) white fish, skin on but scaled and boned (coley is great)

2 tbsp olive oil

¾ spring onions, trimmed and cut in to thin slices

1 tin 400ml low-fat coconut milk

1 fresh red chilli, finely sliced

4 tomatoes halved and de-seeded (optional)

Fresh coriander, leaves picked, stalks finely chopped

1 lemon, cut into wedges

1 cup basmati rice

Sea salt

Cooking time and prep - less than half an hour

Method:

Spread approximately one tablespoon of curry paste all over the flesh side of the fish fillets. Add the olive oil to the large frying pan and heat, then add the fish flesh-side down to the pan and cook for about ten minutes, turning halfway.

Turn the heat up slightly and add most of the sliced spring onions and fresh chillies, coriander stalks and tomatoes. Immediately add the remaining curry paste and the coconut milk. Simmer for a couple of minutes until the fish is starting to flake apart. Remove from the heat and taste the curry sauce; add a squeeze of lemon juice if required.

While the curry is cooking, add one cup of rice to a small pan with two cups of boiling water and a pinch of salt (optional). Bring to the boil and simmer for seven to eight minutes. When all the water is absorbed, remove from the heat and cover with a cloth to keep warm, this will also help it stay "fluffy".

Serve the curry with basmati rice and naan bread. Add remaining spring onions, chilli and coriander leaves to garnish.

Lee Moreton

Prince's Trust supported young person – Enterprise

Smoked Dorset chaps and warm cannellini bean salad

When I moved to secondary school, I started to mix with the wrong crowd and my attendance and grades slipped. I got into some 'naughty stuff' and fell out with my family.

I realised that the only way I would be able to change was to move away from the people that I had been mixing with and start a new somewhere else. I then enrolled at college where I met, my now fiancée, Tara. She gave me more focus and also slapped me with an ultimatum between her or the drugs! A hard decision but I chose the most expensive and promised to clean up.

After completing the course, I worked at various butcher shops until I ended up at an organic farm shop and butchery.

Unfortunately the farm shop went into liquidation and Ben (my current business partner) and I both lost our jobs. It felt like I was back to square one, but Ben had an idea (uh oh). He suggested that we start our own company producing Charcuterie. We attended the four day Prince's Trust business course and were assigned a mentor, who helped us secure a loan and set up The Dorset Chacuterie Company. Without this help we would probably still be on job seekers allowance!

I have now taken up teaching Butchery and Chacuterie at White Pepper Cookery School in Dorset.

Ingredients

Serves 4 as a starter, 2 as a main

4 packs / 8 slices of smoked Dorset chaps

2 good handfuls of seasonal greens, kale, kalvo nero or sea beet (stalks removed)

1 tin of cannellini / butter beans

150ml good organic chicken stock

100ml double cream

1 tbsp fresh young thyme (chopped)

1 tbsp fresh chives (chopped)

2 heaped tsp 'From Dorset With Love' wholegrain mustard

1 tbsp seasoned flour

½ tsp caraway seeds

1 good knob of butter

A good drizzle of 'Green Weald' Rapeseed oil

A small handful of dried apple crisps

Method:

Toast caraway seeds in pan before adding butter to melt. Add kale to pan and cook with a little of the chicken stock until wilted slightly.

Drain beans then transfer to another saucepan with the remaining chicken stock, cook until liquid reduces slightly before adding cream and reduce further until thickened. Finish with the thyme and chives. Season to taste. You are looking for a nice thick sauce consistency.

Flour slices of chaps and fry lightly in rapeseed oil until golden brown and slightly rendered.

Place the beans at the bottom of the dish with plenty of sauce, add the kale in the middle and then chaps on top of this!

Dress with a neat drizzle of rapeseed oil and a few apple crisps.

Les Ferdinand

Football

Beans on toast with grilled chicken

This was the meal that I ate prior to scoring the 10,000th goal in the Premier League. It was during my time at Tottenham Hotspur and in a game against Fulham.

I would cook this meal and eat it prior to a game as it provides the required nutrients, carbohydrates and protein.

Ingredients

Serves 1

A large skinless chicken breast

A 415g tin of baked beans

2 rounds of multigrain bread (at least)

Method:

Cook the chicken under a hot grill until nice and golden. Heat the beans in a medium sized saucepan, stirring occasionally.

Toast the bread, plate up and add the chicken and beans!

In order to get maximum energy, wash down with a protein shake.

Lizzie Simmonds

Swimming

Sweet potato soup

I relate this dish to winning because although a bowl of soup could be considered a small and insignificant meal, this one packs a surprising punch, making it a definite winner for lunch and dinner! I think I see myself a bit like this - I may not be as big or bold as some of my competitors but I'm still one to watch!

Elizabeth Simmonds, aged 21, competes in the 100 / 200m backstroke. She has competed at the European, Commonwealth and World Championships. Lizzie was the European Champion 2010, a Commonwealth medalist in 2010 and also competed at Beijing Olympic Games.

Ingredients

1 butternut squash, peeled, cored and chopped into rough cubes

3 medium sweet potatoes, peeled and chopped into similar cubes

3 or 4 medium carrots, washed and chopped into similar chunks as the other veg

4 cloves of garlic, skin still on

1 white onion, finely chopped

3 or 4 chillies finely chopped - this can be altered, depending how spicy you like your soup

1l chicken stock

1l vegetable stock

Olive oil

Method:

Throw the butternut squash, sweet potato, carrots and garlic (make sure the cloves are still in their skins or they will burn!) onto a couple of baking trays, splash over some olive oil and stick in a pre-heated oven (at around 200°C) for around forty-five minutes. Have a check every twenty minutes or so, giving them a shake each time. They should be lovely and soft and cooked all the way through.

Meanwhile put the onion and chilies in a frying pan with a little olive oil and cook on a medium heat until soft and golden brown. If they seem like they're catching, turn the heat down a little.

Prepare the stock – I use the Knorr jellied stock cubes that you just add boiling water to - and leave to cool slightly.

When everything is out of the oven, line them up next to your blender. It's best to wait five to ten minutes at this stage or things can get pretty heated when you throw it all in!

Find the garlic cloves amongst your roast veg. Use a sharp knife to snip off the very end of each, and then squeeze each clove out of it's skin. Add the clove back to your veg mix and discard the skins.

When you're ready to go, get a large spoon, or preferably a pair of kitchen tongs, and start adding your roast vegetables to the blender. When it's about half full, add about half of one of your stocks, and some of the onion mix, and then blitz. Keep repeating this until your blender is full, then decant to a large pan and do the rest of the veg. To be honest it doesn't really matter which order you blend your veg, or add your stock - it's all going to be mixed together in the end! The stock levels are guidelines - if you prefer your soup a little runnier then add a bit more, if you prefer it thicker then leave some out. It's such an easy recipe that you really can make it your own! When everything has been blended and added together, just heat through on the stove and season well and your soup is ready to serve. You should end up with a lovely smooth soup, full of flavour and with a real warmth from the chilli!

Martin Castrogiovanni

Rugby Union

Carbonara

Delicious home made Italian dishes, in a stylish setting, with new ownership by Leicester Tigers players Geordan Murphy and Martin Castrogiovanni in Leicester and Market Harborough.

One of the most recognisable faces – and frames – in rugby, Martin Castrogiovanni passed 100 appearances for Leicester Tigers during his fifth season at the club in 2010/11.

Born in Argentina, he moved to Italy to pursue his rugby career and made his international debut for the Azzurri against New Zealand in 2002. An ever-present in the World Cups of 2003 and 2007, he scored a try in his 50th Test during the 2008 Six Nations and is now one of the most-capped players in the country's history.

Known as 'Castro', the immensely popular tighthead played against Tigers four times in his spell with Calvisano before landing at Welford Road in 2006.

He made an immediate impact on English rugby, being named Premiership Player of the Year in 2006/07, the first prop and first Italian to receive that honour, as well as picking up EDF Energy Cup and Premiership winners' medals.

He won a second Premiership title in 2009, though missed the final for a second time due to injury, and played in the Heineken Cup Final against Leinster at Murrayfield that year.

Castro finally started a Premiership Final in 2010 as Tigers beat Saracens, and claimed the club's Try of the Season award for his popular interception score against London Irish at Welford Road.

Ingredients

Serves 4

400g spaghetti

200g pancetta cubes

75g parmesan (more to serve) - grated

2 large eggs

100g double cream

3 shallots – small cubes

1 tbsp olive oil

1 clove of garlic grated

Method:

Boil the spaghetti.

Meanwhile, in a pan (quite large as will add the spaghetti in here) fry in oil the pancetta, garlic and shallots on a medium heat.

In a bowl mix the eggs, cream and cheese and whisk until a smooth texture – season with salt and pepper.

Once spaghetti is done, drain and add to pan and on a high heat add the egg/cream/cheese mixture and blitz for a couple of minutes.

Season to taste and serve immediately!

Martyn Williams

Rugby Union

Breakfast for champions

This is my pre-match breakfast that I have had before every game for the last fifteen years!

Its one which my mother would make me the morning of games when I was living at home.

Even though my preparation for matches has changed over the years this one recipe has remained a constant and seen me to two Grand Slams and three British and Irish Lions tours.

Ingredients

Serves 1

4 rashers of organic bacon

3 organic scrambled eggs

Small tin of baked beans

2 pieces of wholemeal toast

2 oven grilled tomatoes – for about 5 mins

Handful of button mushrooms – pan fried

Method:

Grill the bacon, scramble the eggs,
heat the beans – you know what to do –
it's a breakfast!

Michaela Breeze

Weightlifting

Salmon and sweet potato

This is one of my favourite meals. Not only is it high in protein, which I need to help recovery from intense power training sessions.

There is so much goodness in all of the ingredients. A mixture of normal potatoes with sweet potatoes adds variety and stacks of goodness. At the end of the day, you would only put the best quality fuel in to a racing car, I try to treat my body the same way.

Ingredients

1 salmon

1 large potato

1 large sweet potato

A handful of broccoli

1 carrot

1 corn on the cob

2 - 3 tsp green pesto

Ground black pepper or cajun seasoning

Olive oil

Utensils

Tin foil

2 baking trays

Steamer or saucepan

Method:

Prepare the potatoes by dicing into small cubes. Sweet potatoes are a 'super food' and are a great food to include in your diet. Their nutritional values are significantly better than normal potatoes.

Place diced potatoes on a baking tray and pour a small amount of olive oil over. Olive oil is better than vegetable or sunflower oil.

Sprinkle with either black pepper or cajun spice and toss before placing in oven on gas mark 8 for forty minutes.

Prepare the salmon by spreading green pesto generously over the top of the salmon.

Loosely wrap salmon in tin foil and place on bottom shelf of the oven for twenty minutes. Make sure the potatoes have had a twenty minute head start and toss them before adding the salmon. (If cooking the salmon separately from potatoes, I suggest a lower temperature, maybe gas mark 6 for twenty-five minutes).

Chop carrots and broccoli and steam for fifteen minutes. Alternatively if no steamer is available then boil for fifteen minutes. It is best to serve the veg a little crunchy as it keeps more of the goodness in. Soggy veg will have lost most of its nutrients.

Once cooked, serve the salmon, potatoes and veg and enjoy Michaela Breeze's favourite meal.

Neil Mallender

Cricket / Umpiring

Tomato soup poured over chips with poached eggs

Neil Mallender received his big chance late in life, and seized the opportunity wonderfully well. He was selected for England at the age of 30 to play against Pakistan in 1992. He took 5 for 50 and eight wickets in the match (the best figures by an English debutant for nine years), helping to win the game.

Mallender was born in Yorkshire, but began his first-class career for Northamptonshire in 1980, having impressed on a tour of the West Indies with England Young Cricketers. A right-arm fast-medium bowler, and an increasingly useful lower-order batsman, he was capable of bowling at a sharp pace. He won his county cap in 1984 and moved to Somerset in 1987. He was an important part of the rebuilding process at Taunton. He had come close to selection twice previously for England, both times in New Zealand, when the touring side were struggling with injuries.

He became a respected first-class umpire, having been appointed to the list in 1999, and quickly rose through the ranks to stand in his first one-day international when England played Pakistan at Lord's in 2001. He made his umpiring Test debut at Lahore in October 2003.

This recipe got Neil through early childhood, then served him well after long days bowling. This recipe caused him much amusement in Australia when other players could not understand tomato soup poured over chips.

Ingredients

Serves 4-6 people

For the chips

600g Maris Piper potatoes – or as many as you'd like!

180ml cooking oil

(Or could deep fat fry instead, follow cooking instructions)

For the tomato soup

1kg ripe tomatoes, washed and cut into quarters, (optional tin of plum tomatoes)

1 onion – chopped small pieces

2 carrots – chopped small pieces

2 tbsp olive oil

2 tbsp tomato puree

1 tsp sugar

2 bay leaves

2 vegetable stock cubes – 2 pints made with hot water

For the poached eggs

8 eggs

Method:

Scrub the potatoes and cut into thick chunky chips (don't peel them) and then rinse in cold water.

Remove excess water and rub the oil over the chips, so all are covered.

Put on the oven at 200˚C for about forty-five minutes, turn a couple of times.

Heat the oil in a large pan on a low heat, add the carrots and onion and stir. Leave for about ten minutes until soft, keep stirring frequently.

Add the tomato puree and mix in, then add the tomatoes (if adding the tinned tomatoes and them now). Add the sugar, two bay leaves and black pepper to taste and give it a good mix.

Put the lid on and cook for ten minutes and stir a couple of times.

Slowly pour and stir in the vegetable stock simultaneously, increase the heat and then bring to boil. Put the lid on and turn back down to low heat, leave for thirty minutes (or until tomatoes have broken down). Stir every ten minutes or so.

Remove the bay leaves and ladle the soup into a blender to make into a puree, do not over-fill so repeat as many times as you need.

Reheat the pureed soup for five minutes on a low heat, season to taste.

Put 1cm of water into a frying pan, bring to boil and then crack an egg (or however many fit in) and cook four mins or until the egg white has turned white.

Neil Robinson

Table Tennis

Chilli con carne

Seven time Paralympian, seven Paralympic medals, Former European champion, Former World No.1 and Current GB Paralympics Table Tennis coach.

This recipe 'rocks', it's the best chilli recipe in the world. I love it because it brings me together with my wife, Karen and daughter, Emily for happy times. Serve it with fresh crusty bread, fresh rocket or tossed salad and some homemade guacamole.

Ingredients

Serves 4 people

2 medium onions

2 cloves of garlic

Olive oil

2 level tsp chilli powder

1 fresh red chilli, deseeded and finely chopped

1 heaped tsp ground cumin

Sea salt and freshly ground black pepper

455g / 1lb best minced beef

200g / 7oz sun-dried tomatoes, in oil

2 x 400g / 14oz tins of tomatoes

1 x 400g / 14oz tin of red kidney beans, drained

For the guacamole

1 ripe avocado, peeled and chopped

¼, onion, peeled, finely chopped

½, lemon, juice only

Salt and freshly ground black pepper

1 deseeded tomato, chopped

Method:

Use a large pan to cook this dish.

Blitz the onions and garlic in a food processor until finely chopped then fry in a little olive oil until soft. Add the chilli powder, fresh chilli, cumin and a little seasoning, give it a good stir.

Then add the minced beef and continue to cook, stirring, until browned. Blitz the sun-dried tomatoes in the food processor with enough oil from the jar to loosen into a paste.

Add a wine glass measure of water and two tins of tomatoes, season a little more if required.

I lace it with black pepper mmmm! Bring to the boil, cover with greased proof paper and the lid then turn down the heat to simmer and cook for one and a half hours.

Add the drained kidney beans thirty minutes before the end of the cooking time. It tastes much better if you cook it the day before, keep it in the fridge and the tastes will develop.

To make the guacamole, mash the avocado in a big dish, mix in the onion, squeeze the lemon juice and the tomato into the mix and combine. Season to taste...lovely!

Nick Gillingham

Swimming

Parma ham and melon
Calves liver with mashed potato, peas and gravy
Lemon sorbet

I really like fruit, melon is so thirst quenching and with Parma ham it just adds that point of difference that winning needs. I really like the taste of liver, that tangy almost slightly sour taste and when cooked to perfection it melts in your mouth. I'm very much a meat and two veg person, so the mashed potato and peas give me that health factor.

I still have a very busy lifestyle and I need lots of energy so the complex carbohydrate in the potato gives me lasting energy.

The protein in the liver gives me iron and helps my muscles recover after a hectic day with the children or after a run or swim. Finally, the sharp lemon sorbet is so zesty that my mouth feels alive and I feel fresh, all in all it's a great winning meal.

Ingredients

For the melon and Parma ham

1 ripe cantaloupe melon

120g Parma ham

Balsamic vinegar (optional)

For the calves liver with mashed potato, peas and gravy

1 tbsp plain flour

400g calves livers cut into slices

20g unsalted butter

2 tbsp olive oil

2 tbsp white wine vinegar

Mashed potatoes

800g Maris Piper / King Edward potatoes – peeled, washed and cut into chunks

¼ pint full fat / semi skimmed milk

Salt and freshly ground pepper to taste

For the lemon sorbet

1 ¼ cup caster sugar

1 ¼ cup water

Juice of 5 – 6 lemons (medium sized)

Rind of 2 lemons or about 3 tsp

Method:

For the melon and Parma ham

Cut and de-seed the melon into slices or wedges (roughly five inches) and peel the skin.

Wrap each melon piece with Parma ham.

Drizzle with some balsamic vinegar and serve.

For the calves liver and mash

Heat the oil and butter in a large frying pan on a medium to high heat. Dust the liver in the flour and sauté quickly until brown in colour yet tender. Stir in the white wine vinegar and mix together.

Bring potatoes to boil in a large pan and then on a medium heat with the lid on simmer for about twenty minutes or when easily ready to mash. Warm the milk either in a pan or microwave.

Place the potatoes in a bowl, rinse, drain, and start mashing. Add the milk and mash until smooth, add salt and pepper.

Serve with peas!

For the lemon sorbet

On a high heat mix the sugar and water until slightly bubbling, it will form a syrup. Take off heat and allow cooling completely.

Once cooled, add lemon juice and zest and leave to chill in the fridge.

Once completely chilled, freeze in an ice cream maker (follow instructions) or blast in a chiller.

Place sorbet in an airtight container and put in the freezer.

Serve when needed!

Rebecca Adlington

Swimming

Banana and chocolate cake

I love a 'little' slice of this after training or when it's freshly baked and still warm. I make my own on a regular (very regular) basis and I often make it for other people too as it's so yummy.

This is my favourite recipe, I hope you like it.

Ingredients

3 bananas – mashed up with a fork

2 eggs

75g butter

1 tsp baking soda

¼ tsp baking powder

½ tsp salt

225g sugar

200g plain flour

80ml water

100g Cadbury's dairy milk chocolate – chopped into chunks

100g chopped walnuts – optional

A pinch of brown sugar – for decoration

Method:

Preheat your oven to 180°C and line a loaf tin with greaseproof paper. Next whisk together your sugar and butter in a large bowl. Add in the eggs, bananas and water and whisk well.

Sift in the flour, bicarbonate of soda, baking powder and salt and then whisk again. Stir in the chocolate and walnuts (if using), then add the mixture to your loaf tin and sprinkle brown sugar onto the top.

Bake for one hour or until a skewer comes out clean and it's cooked through.

Robert Welbourn

Swimming

Energy bars

Robert Welbourn is one of the very few British swimmers to win medals at all the major games, Paralympics, World and European Championships and Commonwealth Games.

At both the Athens and Beijing Summer Paralympics, he won gold medals in the 4x100m relay and in the 400 metre freestyle events he won silver. Rob has qualified to compete in the 2012 Olympics in the S10 freestyle 400m!

Wendy (Rob's mum) makes batches of energy bars to make sure he's getting the essential foods to refuel him after a heavy training session. These "homemade" ones are not only packed with obvious energy giving vitamins, minerals, fibre and carbohydrates, they taste good too.

Ingredients

200g oats

100g dried skimmed milk

100g dried apricots

150g raisins / sultanas

100g walnuts

25g sesame seeds

25g pumpkin seeds

100g brown sugar

100g honey

150g peanut butter

2 drops vanilla essence

1 ½ tbsp vegetable oil
(to help it all bind)

Method:

Preheat the oven to 180˚C.

Chop all the ingredients into small pieces.

Mix all the ingredients together in a
large bowl.

Place in a greased baking tin.

Bake for ten to fifteen minutes at 180˚C.

Take out and leave to cool for about thirty
minutes, then cut to divide it up into bars.

Roger Black

Athletics – 400 metres

Chicken and butternut squash risotto

Roger has won individual silver medals in the 400 metres sprint at both the Olympic Games and World Championships, two individual gold medals at the European Championships, and 4x400 metres relay gold medals at both the World and European Championships.

My signature dish is chicken and butternut squash risotto; I cooked this on Celebrity Masterchef. It's a great dish to throw together when you're hosting a dinner party, it's quick and tasty and you can spend more time with your guests!

Ingredients

Serves 4 people

Knob of butter

2 tbsp olive oil

1 onion – finely chopped

1 inch ginger - grated

Butternut squash

3 chicken breasts – cut into cubes

1 vegetable stock cube

12 oz risotto rice – mixed with hot water approx 1 litre

Mix in parmesan to taste

Ciabatta to serve

Method:

Chop squash into chunks, de-seed, peel and cut into quarters and drizzle honey over the squash – oven roast 180˚C for approx forty minutes or until soft.

Cook the chicken in one tablespoon olive oil in a pan and then set aside.

Fry (on a medium heat) one tablespoon oil, the butter and onions in a large saucepan, until onions have browned.

Add risotto rice, cook for about four minutes, in the meantime crumble the stock cube in a litre of hot water and mix together.

Ladle a spoonful of stock mixture into the risotto, wait till the all the water has been absorbed and then repeat this process until all mixture has been used.

Then mix the squash and chicken into the risotto, add parmesan and set aside for two minutes before serving.

Scott Alderdice

Prince's Trust supported young person – Get Into

Fettuccine alla carbonara

My name is Scott and I am 26 years old. Before I got involved with The Prince's Trust I had come out of one year rehabilitation in Spain from a heroin addiction.

Aged 21, I lived on the streets of London for about two years. I came back to Northern Ireland and tried to find work, but found it really difficult. When I was signing on one day, I saw the poster for the Get Into Youth Work programme.

The programme was brilliant from the first day, and by the end of it you really felt like you were amongst brothers and sisters. The experience helped my confidence in group settings so much. I applied for a 30 hour per week Peer Support worker post with Youth Action, and I was successful.

From The Prince's Trust programme, I have gained so much confidence to apply for work and experiences I would not have done before.

I also work for Council for the Homeless, where I facilitate training in CPR and how to combat overdose. In addition, I work as a chef in a local Belfast restaurant.

As you can see I am a very busy young man, who is very happy with the varied types of employment opportunities I have gained with the help of the initial start from The Prince's Trust.

Ingredients

3 fresh porcini mushrooms
(or 1 ounce of dried porcini mushrooms)

2 tbsp extra-virgin olive oil

1 tbsp dry white vermouth

300g pancetta

1 or 2 medium white onions - medium diced

6 medium garlic cloves - minced

¾ cup heavy cream

500g fettuccine (can substitute linguine)

75g parmesan - grated for garnish

4 tbsp Italian parsley -
chopped for garnish

Method:

If using fresh mushrooms, clean the dirt off all surfaces; cut off and discard the base of the stems. Separate the stems from the caps and thinly slice everything. Combine sliced mushrooms with one tablespoon of the olive oil and the vermouth; set aside to macerate for thirty minutes.

If using dried mushrooms, combine them in a small bowl with one tablespoon of the olive oil and the vermouth. Cover mixture with warm water and set aside for thirty minutes to reconstitute mushrooms.

Cut pancetta slices into quarter inch squares. Heat remaining olive oil in a large frying pan over medium - high heat. When oil shimmers, add pancetta and cook, stirring occasionally, until browned, about ten minutes.

Add mushroom mixture (with liquid), onion, and garlic to pancetta. Reduce heat to medium and simmer until garlic and onions are soft and sauce is slightly reduced.

Once mixture has reduced, lower heat to medium low, add cream, and let it simmer for five minutes more, then set aside.

Cook pasta according to the package directions. Meanwhile, re-warm the sauce over low heat. When the pasta is cooked, drain it, return it to the stockpot, add sauce and mix well.

Garnish with grated parmesan and parsley to serve.

Shane Williams
Rugby Union

Corned beef pie

Shane is a leading International Rugby Union test try scorer. He earned his first cap for Wales at the age of 22 against France in the 1999-2000 Six Nations season. In this tournament, on his first full start he scored a try against Italy.

He has been part of two Grand Slam winning teams in 2005 and 2008. In 2005 he scored tries against England, Italy and Scotland, surpassing this in 2008 with tries against Scotland, Ireland, France and two against Italy.

Ingredients

1 small onion

2 ½ lb Welsh potatoes with salted butter and a tbsp of milk

1 ½ tins of corned beef

Large pinch of paprika

Salt and pepper

Method:

Chop the onion finely and sauté until soft and translucent.

Add the salt, pepper and paprika and stir.

Chop the corned beef into small chunks and add to the onion.

Stir the corned beef into the mashed potato and place in an oven proof dish.

Sprinkle the grated cheese on top and place in an oven on gas mark 5 until golden brown.

One of my favourite meals is corned beef pie.

Yummy!

Shaun Wane

Rugby League

Kleftico

Whenever I invite the players round for food, this is a meal I cook for them as its simple, nourishing and leaves enough time to have plenty of banter as it cooks. It's a tasty no hassle dish, enjoy!

Ingredients

400g diced lamb

1 tbsp oregano

120g feta cheese cubed

250ml white wine

6 baby tomatoes

50g chorizo chopped

2 medium cubed potatoes

4 finely chopped shallots

4 cloves of garlic chopped

Method:

Take a piece of baking paper, double it up and place in an oven proof dish.

Simply add the ingredients, seal as a parcel as tight as possible ensuring none of the flavours escape!

Cook slowly for four hours in a pre-heated 180°C (gas mark 4) oven.

No hassle and tastes great!

Steven Gerrard

Football

Chicken and broccoli fusilli with flaked almonds

One of the most prolific players ever to wear the famous red shirt, Steven Gerrard has spent his whole career at Liverpool.

He made his debut during the 1998 season and became club Captain in 2003.

He has won FA Cups, League Cups, a UEFA cup and Super Cups. However, arguably his best achievement was to captain the side to a famous Champions League victory in Istanbul against AC Milan in 2005.

The win was significant as it was the club's fifth time it had won the trophy. This meant that it would remain at Anfield for evermore.

Ingredients

Serves 2 people

350g fusilli pasta

300g broccoli, cut into small florets

1 tsp virgin olive oil

3 large skinless, boneless chicken breasts cut into chunks

2 garlic cloves, crushed

25g flaked almonds

Method:

Cook the fusilli in a large pan of boiling water, adding salt to taste.

After five minutes add the broccoli for a further three minutes until cooked.

Whilst the pasta is cooking, gently heat the oil in a large frying pan or wok. Add the chicken and stir occasionally. After eight minutes, add the crushed garlic and continue cooking until the chicken pieces are golden.

Take a small frying pan and lightly toast the almonds.

Drain the pasta and broccoli and toss in the chicken, then top off with almonds.

Season well and serve.

Tideswell School of Food

Tideswell School of Food lies at the heart of the Taste Tideswell project – a community led social enterprise that aims to stimulate the local economy by transforming its food economy. The village won funding support from the BIG Lottery Fund and was featured in the BBC One Village SOS programme in September 2011.

Tideswell School of Food is a resource for local people as well as a professionally run cookery school. The facilities and experts at the school help to teach people of all ages and backgrounds how to grow, cook, make, brew, and sell food and drink.

Anyone who comes on a course at the Tideswell School of Food is supporting our wider aims and objectives – thank you to everyone who does support us this way. As a not-for-profit organisation, we plough back all surpluses into our business and educational programmes. We buy everything as locally as we can, employ local people, and support local enterprises as much as possible.

Thank you

We'd like to say a special thank you to all those who helped to prepare all the food for the publication over the two days. The names of the volunteers are listed below:

Judy Cooke
Michelle Lindley
Carrie Warr
Tricia Vernon
Lynda Sneddon
Nadeen Plumtree
Kate Lyon
Tina Edwards
Elaine Kearney
Maureen Douglas
Margaret Coterill
Elaine Taylor Fisher
Juliet Waugh
Kim Wathall
Sallie Challupa

Find out more

To find out more about Tideswell School of Food or to view the full list of cookery courses available visit us at:

www.tideswellschooloffood.co.uk

01298 871262

info@tideswellschooloffood.co.uk

Follow us:

Twitter - @TideswellFood

Facebook - Tideswell School of Food

Tideswell School of Food
The Courtyard
Commercial Road
Tideswell
Derbyshire
SK17 8NY

Prince's Trust

The Prince's Trust

There are more than one million young people in the UK not in education, employment or training. The Prince's Trust focuses its efforts on those young people who need our help the most. We help develop key skills, confidence and motivation, enabling young people to move into work, education or training.

Programmes to support young people

- We run programmes that encourage young people to take responsibility for themselves – helping them build the life they choose rather than the one they've ended up with.

- The Enterprise Programme provides money and support to help young people start up in business.

- The Team Programme is a 12-week personal development course, offering work experience, qualifications, practical skills, community projects and a residential week.

- Get into's are short courses offering intensive training and experience in a specific sector to help young people get a job.

- Development Awards are small grants to enable young people to access education, training or work.

- XL clubs give 13-19 year olds who are at risk of truanting, exclusion and underachievement a say in their education. They aim to improve attendance, motivation and social skills.

Raising funds

The Prince's Trust needs to raise almost £1 million a week to continue its vital work. We rely upon generous donations and fundraising from a huge variety of people and partners.

We are proud of our longstanding partnership with Lafarge. By working together, we can ensure that our partnerships can continue to strive towards improving the lives of more young people who need help and support to achieve their potential.

For more information about The Prince's Trust:

Visit our website www.princes-trust.org.uk

Give us a call 020 7543 1234

Proud to support
The Prince's Trust

Helping to create brighter futures for young people is part of Lafarge's commitment to local communities. That's why we support organisations like The Prince's Trust, which helps young people overcome barriers to gain employment, training or education opportunities.

Lafarge UK is a major supplier of innovative concretes, cements, aggregates and asphalts plus waste management services. Lafarge is proud of its hands-on approach to sustainability, from quarry restoration and nature conservation to recycling, product development and alternative transport.

For more information please call:
0844 561 0037
www.lafarge.co.uk
www.facebook.com/LafargeUK

LAFARGE

bringing materials to *life* ™

creative**triangle** ◀

We have all the ingredients you need for the perfect design solution.

Whisk our fresh and friendly design consultants together with our talented graphic designers to unlock the aroma of sweet success.

Add a splash of our vintage 15 years' experience to the mix, together with a sprinkling of cost effectiveness.

You should now have flexible pasta dough that can be shaped into a variety of creative solutions to fit a varied market.

To cook, just pop us into a pan of boiling water – don't worry we can handle the heat!

From initial ideas to a delicious design in no time at all, we are the perfect option if you're in need of a well-rounded meal.

For a taste of who we are please visit our website or contact us.

www.creativetriangle.co.uk

enquiries@creativetriangle.co.uk

0116 253 3408

Salmon and lemon pansotti (triangular shaped pasta) in a white wine and cream sauce.

Tristanpoyser photography

Award winning photographer Tristan Poyser, has over ten years commercial experience with clients including Nike and Lafarge.

Although a specialist within Architecture and Sports he has a huge passion for food photography, so when approached to shoot for this great cause he jumped at the opportunity. The creative direction, was undertaken by Suelen Wong. Suelen has a solid background within advertising and marketing for some of the UK's most loved brands and has worked in partnership with Tristan on many successful projects. This strong relationship ensured that 40 plus recipes were shot successfully over the two-day sessions.

Their exciting partnership has continued where they have collaborated on other creative photographic projects both at home and abroad, including ongoing projects on food within the Far East.

For more information about Tristan and Suelen

Email: tristan@tristanpoyser.co.uk

Web: www.tristanpoyser.co.uk

Twitter: twitter.com/tristanpoyser

Bene Factum Publishing

An independent British non-fiction publisher.

Bene Factum specialises in publishing biographies, business, cookery, general information, classic travel writing and company histories. Our list is constantly evolving with new and interesting books.

In these days of big publishing conglomerates, Bene Factum believes that smaller is beautiful. We are convinced that the way to produce and sell good books is to give our authors the personal service that will make their books stand out in competitive market places – national and international.

Our very high production values ensure we deliver the best books that an independent publisher can deliver.

Many Bene Factum books are highly illustrated, and some are bespoke, co-operative or sponsored project.

You are welcome to buy any of our books on our list directly from this website…and keep an eye out for special offers.

Bene Factum Publishing
PO Box 58122
London
SW8 5WZ
Tel: 020 7720 6767

Email: inquiries@bene-factum.co.uk
www.bene-factum.co.uk

Geoff Neal Litho is an award winning quality printing and direct mail company based near Heathrow

When asked to help with this project we had no hesitation. We believe in the inspirational work of the Trust.

At Geoff Neal litho Limited we love print and direct mail. We enjoy coming to work and this comes across in the way we do business. We have a strong reputation built up since 1976 for high quality work produced on time and at a fair price. We also believe in and take our environmental responsibility very seriously, which can be seen in the credentials we hold.

For more information:

0208 751 4455

www.geoffneallitho.co.uk

NUMBER 1 FOR SERVICE

BIRMINGHAM
0121 322 6650

BRISTOL
01179 387100

CHARLTON
020 8858 6166

FARNBOROUGH
01252 379900

MANCHESTER
0161 868 1200

LITTLEHAMPTON
01903 722122

NEWCASTLE
0161 868 1200

SHEFFIELD
0114 2842000

WATFORD
01923 859944

ELLIOTT BAXTER & COMPANY LIMITED
the UK's leading Independent Paper Supplier

www.ebbpaper.co.uk

EBB 90 years 1922 - 2012

PAPER

Index

Conversion Tables

Weight - imperial to metric

½ oz = 10g
1 oz = 25g
3 oz = 75g
1 lb = 450g
3 lb = 1.35kg

Volume - imperial to metric

2 fl oz = 55ml
5 fl oz / ¼ pint = 150 ml
10 fl oz / ½ pint = 275 ml
1 pint = 750 ml
1 ¾ pints = 1 litre

American cup

1 cup of flour = 5 oz = 150g
1 cup of butter = 8 oz = 225g
1 cup of caster sugar = 8 oz = 225g

Spoon measures

1 level tbsp flour = 15g flour
1 heaped tbsp flour = 28g flour
1 level tbsp sugar = 28g sugar
1 level tbsp butter = 15g butter

Oven temperatures

Gas mark 3 = 325˚F = 170˚C
Gas mark 4 = 350˚F = 180˚C
Gas mark 5 = 375˚F = 190˚C
Gas mark 6 = 400˚F = 200˚C
Gas mark 7 = 425˚F = 220˚C